principles
OF
Success

By Dr. Emmanuel C. Ngoh

Q

QUOTES & PRAISES

Real Lives ... Changed.

"You have been able to influence my life through your book" ~**Wung Evans**

"In your book, I have seen how my faith can be strengthened and rebuilt ... how to solve my own problems ... how to take courage and risk." ~**Ndonwi Shu**

"Your book gives one inspiration and a reason to hope for a better future." ~**Laurean Ajong**

"I think it has enriched my spiritual life." ~**Fomunung Emmanuel**

"As a result of reading this book, I have written down my goals, started eliminating bad habits, and I am clinging more to the Lord." ~**Atanga Sylvon N.**

"I feel blessed by your book. It strengthens my life spiritually and physically."
~*Yefor Caroline*

"I see that what we have been missing is God. I want to understand Him and most of all serve Him."
~*Ayafor Roland Chebefuh*

"After I read your book, I believe strongly in prayer. I would like to know God more and more. Your book also helped me stop smoking." ~*Chingang Kimbeng*

"We have chewed and digested your book. We do not wish to be victims of circumstances any more."
~*Michael Enyenga and Agbor Emmanuel*

"I am inspired by the book. I found answers to my problems." ~*Fur Delphine*

"I was richly blessed by your book. I am experiencing a more successful life."
~*Delphine Atabong*

"I have read your book three times. In fact, I will read it monthly to remind myself of the principles. It has encouraged and helped me!"
~*Misty Carter*

"I have to say it is very inspirational and precise." ~*Larry Abangea*

"I was touched and motivated."
~Yvonne Ngobaso

"When I realized my errors, I wept and
prayed for God to forgive me for the past.
I pray that God will give you more zeal
to do more to help young people."
~Vivian Awasum

"With the principles of this book,
I regained my confidence. I decided to
stand up and be responsible for
what is happening to me."
~Neba A. Youmbissi

RECOMMENDATIONS
Professional Opinions

J.C. Mancho
Pharmacist, President PC Health Services

"A principled, Christ-centered approach to problem solving never fails. Dr. Emmanuel Ngoh's book, Principles of Success, based on this truism offers its readers an apt compass for problem resolution."

Rev. Joshua Cheng
Faith Revival End-Time Ministries, Inc.

"In a very matter-of-fact style, as a brother discussing with relations, Dr. Ngoh invites us to examine the hard facts of our earthly existence so that we might be better prepared to meet the Author of Life when the time comes.

Like the dentist he is, Emmanuel knows that pain must be caused to identify the bad tooth before you extract or fill it. He therefore ventures into the truth that we hate to know, while giving us another opportunity to see the relevance of Jesus in our lives.

By the time you finish reading this book, you would have seen your whole life pass before you like a movie. Now you have the opportunity to look back and to determine your future. God bless you all as you read."

Samuel E. Molind, DMD
Director, Global Health Outreach

"Principles of Success contains sound, biblically based words for life that are timeless and transcend every culture worldwide. This book has started many people on the right path to success, which is meaningless unless it is defined in God's terms.

So have your friends and neighbors, even around the world, sense and understand the great joy of knowing Jesus and a life of true success—I would recommend it. It will put joy back into your life as well!"

Jim Scogin
President, The International Link

"As a patient of Dr. Ngoh's endodontic practice, I can say that it takes only moments to see Christ Jesus in his life as well as in this book. Principles of success is a useful tool. It speaks clearly in understandable terms and equips the believer with magnificent insights.

This resource is powerful—especially for people yearning for meaning!"

"Without being time-consuming, Principles of Success takes the reader through a basic but vital process ... a pathway to meeting and building a beautiful and enjoyable relationship with your Creator.

Principles of Success broadened my narrow view of life. I would highly recommend every-one—sick, well, poor, rich, worthy, unworthy—to read it. The book portrays a life-changing experience, taking the reader from grandiose and big things of life (which often lead to failure because they are rarely met) to the simple but often neglected essentials of life ... the most essential and life-changing things."

"I read your book with keen interest, and my conclusion is that it is a treasure."

T

TABLE OF CONTENTS

DEDICATION

To my beloved nephews, nieces and all who look up to me. I pray that this book will direct you to the Source, the Giver of all good things.

a

ACKNOWLEDGEMENTS
Gratefulness & Thanks

Words cannot express my deep gratitude to Ms. Ingrid Williams who, with Spiritual discernment, was able to capture my thoughts and give sustenance to what you are holding in your hand.

I also want to thank my beloved wife Catherine Ngoh (Manyi) who has given me her unconditional and relentless support. Without her, my life would be incomplete.

INTRODUCTION

Why I Wrote This Book...

This book was written to relieve a burden in my heart. Specifically it was written for my nephews and nieces back in Cameroon to whom I am responsible. The e-mails and letters I received from their friends who read the original manuscript have encouraged me to publish this and make it available to you.

There is no originality in my message to you. It is smeared with fingerprints from other books that have influenced me, and woven of principles that are part of my constitution. These words are adapted from books I have read and seminars I have attended in my quest for a Holy life of personal fulfillment.

This book is not a novel and should not be read from that perspective. In the words of Sir Francis Bacon, **"Some books are** *meant to be tested, others to be swallowed and some few to be chewed and digested."* What you are about to read in this book falls under the latter category.

To get the most out of this book, I recommend that you stop at the end of each chapter to reflect on what you have read. Visualize applying the principles and how your life will be changed. Make notes and determine a plan of action to take steps toward making that a reality.

Action Plans are included with each chapter to assist you in your pursuit of success. Take time to write out your thoughts. This is absolutely critical. First of all, your thoughts become clearer when put on paper. Secondly, when you write down your thoughts, you have a permanent record to which you can refer. Finally, the very act of writing out ideas reinforces your commitment to them.

> *"Write the vision and make it plain on tablets that he may run who reads it."*
> *~Habakkuk 2:2*

In the words of AW Tozer, *"the function of a good book is to stand like a signpost, directing the reader towards the*

Truth and Life. It is my prayer that this book will direct you towards Holiness and Joy.

To those of you who are already believers of the Christian message, this book will encourage you in your walk with the Lord. Our belief and faith assure us of eternal rewards in our final destination—rewards springing from our actions on earth and reflected in the treasures we store up in heaven.

If we seek holiness and strive for a Christ-like life, we will find happiness and success as byproducts. My heart bleeds for you and I yearn for you to turn your life around, wake up and enjoy God's given promise to you. To move north is to turn your back on the South. To move toward a spiritual life of Holiness is to turn your back on ungodliness.

> ***"Now godliness with contentment is great gain."***
> ~1 Timothy 6:6

From my perspective, over 90% of the problems that we face are manmade problems which we bring upon ourselves. I know some of you reading this will think that I do not understand, but remember I was born in Cameroon. I spent 10 years (instead of 7) in Primary School, and was an average student in Secondary and Higher School with barely 4 papers and two papers at the Ordinary & Advanced Levels, respectively. A lot of you reading this are far better off than I was at your age and stage in life.

Some of you may say it is because I am in America. But folks, the principles I am about to share with you are universal principles that know no boundaries. Some of you are better off than those abroad. There are opportunities everywhere including Cameroon, Haiti, Honduras, and even where you are.

Sexually transmitted diseases, HIV, poverty, alcohol consumption, cigarette smoking, and adultery are but a few problems that are on the rise. These are signs of unhappiness. Many of these obsessive behaviors are attempts to achieve a substitute from the outside for what is lacking or insufficient in the inside. The irony is that the more one indulges in these habits, the less one finds fulfillment and instead travels a well-worn road to damnation.

All good things come from God. We need to go to our Father and ask for "living water" that will quench our thirst and wash away the guilt and condemnation of sin so we can live a life of holiness. If we seek a Christ-like life, happiness and success will flourish as we develop a true sense of what He has done to provide a good life for us.

I want you to stop now and ask yourself, "Is there a God?" Ask yourself, "If I died this moment, where will I spend eternity?"

It is ludicrous to think that going to church makes you a Christian or going into a garage makes you an automobile. You cannot go to heaven by your good works alone or by attending church every Sunday. The Bible makes it clear in John 14:6 where Jesus said, ***"I am the way, the truth and the life. No one comes to the Father except through me."***

Without God, we are heading for hell on earth and eternal hell beyond the grave, unless we decide to change right now. The principles I am about to share with you will transform your life if you decide to change. If you keep doing what you are doing, you will keep getting what you've been getting and the cycle continues.

Some of you will refer to your failures as a curse by one of your uncles in the village. Some will fault bad luck, and some will say they were not blessed with rich parents. Some of you are even blaming the government, or your environment. But folks, look in the mirror and you will see the reason for your failures or inability to enjoy life to your God-given potential. You have to live a life by design, otherwise you will fail and suffer by default.

If at this point you are feeling bad about yourself, be careful not to be remorseful without repentance. Remorse is wishing you had not acted a certain way because of the unpleasant consequences. Repentance, however, takes it one step further. It asks and receives forgiveness, and uses that forgiveness to make deliberate changes in the direction of your life.

Remember Judas, the disciple who betrayed Jesus. He became remorseful after he realized what he had done and then committed suicide. Peter, on the other hand, after denying Jesus three times was not only remorseful but sought repentance. He grew to become one of the leaders of the early church, wrote two books in the New Testament and died as a martyr.

Do not beat yourself up. Repent and ask forgiveness. Make deliberate changes in your life's direction.

Dear brothers and sisters I invite you to stop your old ways today. Learn from the principles within this book and ask God to help you change your life. Confess your sins to God and start a new life.

Regardless of your past, your future is a clean slate. Today is the beginning of the rest of your life.

"If we confess our sins,
he is faithful and just
and will forgive us our sins
and purify us from all unrighteousness."

~1 John 1:9

PSALM 139:13-14

*You created my
inmost being ...
I am fearfully
and
wonderfully made.*

KNOW YOUR CREATOR

He did not create in vain.

We are not here by accident. God put us here. There is purpose in His creation. There is purpose for your life, and it extends beyond your life on earth into eternity. In the words of late Jim Reeves, ***"This world is not my own, I'm just passing through."***

> *"God so loved the world,*
> *that He gave his one and only son,*
> *that whosoever believes in him*
> *shall not perish but have eternal life."*
> *~John 3:16*

The eternal life is not promised to only those in America or the Jews but to all who believe in Him. God loves us. He does not want us to perish, but to have everlasting life. For us to claim the promise, we must first of all remove sin from our lives.

> **"But the Scripture has
> confined all under sin,
> that the promise by faith in Jesus Christ
> might be given to those who believe."**
> ~*Galatians 3:22 (NKJV)*

> **"Jesus said to him, 'You shall love the
> Lord your God with all your heart,
> with all your soul,
> and with all your mind.
> This is the first and great commandment.
> And the second is like it:
> You shall love your neighbor as yourself.
> On these two commandments
> hang all the Law and the Prophets.' "**
> ~*Matthew 22:37-40*

Love the Lord with all that is in you. This is the greatest and foremost commandment. Secondly, love others as you love yourself.

You cannot serve two masters. Witchcraft or sorcerers are of the devil and you should flee. Any action short of loving God is tantamount to love for the devil.

Many problems we face stem from the fact
that we have failed the commandments of
love. Some of you are asking, "Doc! What
do you want me to do?" I say to you,

- **OBEY** *those two commandments.*
  (Romans 6:16)
  You serve who you obey. It is easy to see
  who or what your master is by the your
  actions. Are they born of love or of self-
  ishness?

  > *"... the love of God is shed abroad
  > in our hearts by the Holy Ghost
  > which is given unto us."*
  > ~*Romans 5:5*

- **PRAY** *to God continually.*
  (Luke 21:36)
  In prayer you can thank and worship
  God, ask for His help, confess your sins,
  and pray for others.

  > *"Be anxious for nothing,
  > but in everything by prayer
  > and supplication with thanksgiving,
  > let your requests be made known to God."*
  > ~*Philippians 4: 6-7*

- **STUDY** *the Bible daily.*
  (2 Timothy 2:15)
  When you study the Bible, you prove

yourself. Studying helps you understand God's Word correctly and keeps you from being ashamed by your life.

> *"Teach me good judgment*
> *and knowledge:*
> *for I have believed thy commandments.*
> *... I will keep thy precepts*
> *with my whole heart."*
> ~*Psalm 119:66,69b*

- **MEET REGULARLY** *with Christians.*
  (Hebrews 10:25)
  God commands that Christians meet regularly for worship, prayer, Bible study, and helping each other. God knows that friends are important, and these kinds of friends strengthen you.

> *"As iron sharpens iron,*
> *so one man sharpens another."*
> ~*Proverbs 27:17 (NIV)*

All of these things will help you to know God intimately and become more like Him. Know God as only you can know Him. Become the person that only you can be!

ACTION PLAN

Chapter 1

- Identify Christians who "Walk the Talk" and make appointments to share with them. List some people below who have this characteristic.

- Make it a point to read at least one verse from the Bible daily. Find one inspiring verse and write it below.

- Go to God in prayer daily. Begin a prayer list of people or situations you would like to pray for beginning today.

- Fellowship with other Christians in the church regularly. If you are not part of a church or do not know other believers well, find a church you can call home and seek out friendships.

2 TIMOTHY 4:2

*Be ready
in season and
out of season.*

PREPAREDNESS

Be Ready! *(2 Timothy 4:2)*

In my world there is no such thing as "LUCK." Maybe it actually exists, but if it does then it is an acronym for **L**aboring **U**nder **C**orrect **K**nowledge. When opportunity meets preparedness, some call it luck. Luck is not the source of success!

> *"Of what use is money in the hand of a fool, since he has no desire to get wisdom."*
> *~Proverbs 17:16*

If you do not program yourself, no amount of money will make you successful. You and I know of folks who came from rich parents who could afford to send them anywhere in the world, but those boys and girls are wretched today.

Condition your body and position yourself to receive the blessing that the Lord has for you. Your body is the most prized possession that you have. Do not abuse your body. For the sisters reading this, your body is not a sex toy. Remember, GOD does not condone premarital sex or adultery. "The wages of sin is death," so says the Bible. Does it occur to you how HIV is transmitted? You and I know people dying from excessive alcohol consumption, sex, prostitution, tobacco etc., but we deny it and call it "slow poison" or witchcraft.

> *"And that servant who knew his master's will, and did not prepare himself or do according to his will, shall be beaten with many stripes."*
> ~Luke 12:47

The wages of sin may not appear as sudden death to your body, but it can bring death to your lifestyle. It deadens your spirit and kills your dreams. Mistakes come back to beat you again and again until you turn your situation around.

> *"Therefore you also be ready, for the Son of Man is coming*

at an hour you do not expect.
Who then is a faithful and wise servant,
whom his master made ruler
over his household,
to give them food in due season?
Blessed is that servant whom his master,
when he comes, will find so doing.
Assuredly, I say to you that
he will make him ruler
over all his goods."
~Matthew 24:44-47

Here is simple, but valuable advice: Whatever business you are in, learn all that you can about your trade. I know of a carpenter from Akum in Bamenda back in Yaounde when I was at the university in 1984.

George only finished primary school but he was determined to better his English and French. He studied English and French on his own and enrolled in "Cour de Soir" (night school) where he earned his O LEVEL (Ordinary) papers.

He came across some missionaries and became a translator because of his fluency in English and French. Today, George is living the American dream in Texas. Do not tell George he was lucky ... he was prepared!

Dear brothers and sisters, be ready for what God has for you. Be prepared and don't count on luck. Stay away from alcohol, illicit sex and tobacco; else tomorrow an old villager will be blamed for your predicament. Remember Eneke the bird in "Things Fall Apart" by Chinua Achebe; "Since men have learned to shoot without missing, he has to learn to fly without perching."

ACTION PLAN

Chapter 2

- Make a list of your long-term goals. Make these goals something you would like to attain within the next five years.

- Make a list of short-term goals you would like to complete in the near future.

- Next to each goal, write down a plan and timeline for how you intend to accomplish the goal.

EPHESIANS 1:11

*In Him we have
obtained an
inheritance
according to
His purpose.*

3

PURPOSE

Knowing Why

If you do not know where you are going, no road will take you there. Everyone has a purpose in life, a unique gift or special talent. When we blend this talent with service to others we will experience success.

Your life purpose is the big dream in which all your other goals play a supporting part. This is what gets you out of bed in the morning. In the words of Peter Hirsch, **"People who know _why_ they are doing something inevitably outperform people who know _how_; people who know how usually work for people who know why."**

Your purpose is the reason for your success. What is your goal? What is your purpose? Write it down. Read it before you go to bed. Ask God to bless you and provide you with spiritual discernment as you search your purpose. You must write it down and have a clear picture to state it in a concise and meaningful manner.

> **"Write the vision and make it plain on tablets, that he may run who reads it."**
> *~Habakkuk 2:2*

When I came to America in 1986, my goal was to become a dentist. People laughed at me because they felt it was impossible, but I stayed with it. I had supporting goals along the way, but my big purpose was Dentistry. The saying, **"Where there is a will, there is a way!"** proved true for me. The "will" provided the "how."

When my friends were frequenting night-clubs, I was studying or working. My desire to have good grades in my transcript gave me the drive to move forward. My goal consumed me. I visited several dentists, sharing with them my goals and asking for advice. I was confident that I would reach my goal.

> **"Jesus said to him, 'If you can believe, all things are possible to him who believes.'"**
> *~Mark 9:23*

You have to have faith in yourself. Confidence gave me an inner glow and pride. I was unpopular at the time, but I did not care. My actions were geared towards achieving my goal. One of my principles at the time was to stay clear of people or things that could pull me away from my goal. Too many people give up too soon but I was not a quitter.

There is a story of a mining company that had invested heavily in equipment to mine gold. With no apparent success, they got tired and frustrated and sold the equipment to a junkyard. The person who bought the equipment went out and studied the abandoned mine, and with persistent digging hit the largest gold discovery in history.

And let us not grow weary
while doing good,
for in due season we shall reap
if we do not lose heart.
Therefore, as we have opportunity,
let us do good to all,
especially to those who are
of the household of faith.
~Galatians 6:9-10

In my opinion, you can be successful in life if you design the life you want and work at it. Develop the talents you have and dedicate them to the service of others and you will find that God is on your side helping you.

Do you have a dream? Go to our Father in Heaven with your request in prayer. Have faith that it is possible and learn all there is to learn about your plan.

If God is for us, who can be against us?
~Romans 8:31

ACTION PLAN

Chapter 3

- For this exercise, pretend you are attending your own funeral. What would people be saying about you? What do you want them to say about you? Write down your answers for each group of people that follows:

- Friends:

- Co-Workers:

- Family Members:

- If you found a difference between what people would say and what you would want them to say about you, identify those areas below. Use this list to make personal goals for growth.

ACTS 4:23

And being let go, they went to their own company ...

4

THE RIGHT COMPANY

Grow Good Friendships

It is said, "a man is judged by the company he keeps." There are lots of losers out there, drinking and running after women, who are good for nothing. They just want to have a good time.

To the sisters: you know of friends who gossip, have illicit sex and fill their lives with other vices. If you are not selective about the company you keep, you will end up like them.

> **"He who walks with the wise grows wise, but a companion of fools suffers harm."**
> *~Proverbs 13:20*

I have a friend who was a virgin. Her friend was an "experienced" girl who was always jumping from tycoon to tycoon. Without her knowledge, this friend had set her up with another tycoon who on this night had left this virgin without option. The result of that night was an unwanted pregnancy.

Run away from the devil and anything that does not glorify God. If you want to unlock your hidden potential, spend your time with people who will stretch you. Find somebody who thinks faster, runs faster, and aims higher. Those are the people who will lift you up.

Where you are now at this moment is a result of choices you have made in the past.

"Circumstances do not make a man. They only reveal him."
James Allen

We grew up with this script "Na condition make Njanga's back to bend." *(Translation: Hardship has made the shrimp's back bent.)* But that is not true. Conditions did not make Njanga's back bend. It only brought out the potential already in Njanga's back to bend.

If you are a thief, don't blame it on poverty. Circumstances only brought out the thief that was in you.

Stop blaming others for your problems and begin to look for answers. If you are a failure, it is because you have let yourself become one. It is not the government's fault. It is not your family's fault. It is no one's fault but your own.

> *"A man can not directly*
> *choose his circumstances,*
> *but he can choose his thoughts,*
> *and so indirectly, yet surely,*
> *shape his circumstances."*
> James Allen

There is a saying that you cannot stop a bird from landing on your head but you can stop it from making a nest.

Stand up and be responsible for what is happening to you. When you do, you create your own opportunity for positive change.

> *"The past is history,*
> *the future is a mystery,*
> *and this moment is a gift.*
> *That is why this moment*
> *is called the present.*

> ***Your past is important,***
> ***but it is not nearly as important***
> ***to your present***
> ***as is the way you see your future."***
>
> **Dr. Tony Campolo**

I try not to waste my time on what is past, because there is nothing I can do about it. I concentrate on the moment ... "What am I doing to improve my tomorrow?" Seek solutions to your problems, not sympathy.

When we go for the solution, we start to see the problem in a different light. Generating self-pity does no good. It holds you to the past. It is far more gratifying to generate admiration instead of pity.

Dwelling in self-pity and blaming someone else is counterproductive. It is a waste of time and energy (along with all forms of resentment, bitterness, and unforgiveness) because the results are negative instead of positive and set you back even further.

You are in the middle and are being pulled on one side by your past and the other side by your future. The choice is yours.

You must either let go of your future and stay with your past, which will generate self-pity, or you can let go of your past and sail with your future to your God-given potential.

> **"The righteous should**
> **choose his friends carefully,**
> **For the way of the wicked**
> **leads them astray."**
>
> *~Proverbs 12:26*

> **"Do not be misled.**
> **Bad company corrupts good character."**
>
> *~1 Corinthians 15:33*

ACTION PLAN

Chapter 4

- Make a list of people with a positive influence. Let them know how you feel about them and gravitate toward them.

- Make a second list of friends with a negative influence who can lead you on the wrong path and stay away from them.

- This is the most difficult and most important part. Declare your new life to the bad company and strictly keep from associating with them. On the other hand, pursue the company of true friends with a positive influence. Also consider finding a mentor or spiritual leader from whom you can learn and be inspired.

LUKE 21:19

*By your patience,
possess your souls.*

DELAYED GRATIFICATION

Patience Brings Peace

Simply put, the principle of delaying gratification means that one hour of pain followed by six hours of pleasure is preferable to one hour of pleasure followed by six hours of pain.

Ask your friends with HIV and they will tell you that the pleasure they first enjoyed was not worth the life they now face with disease.

In the book *The Road Less Traveled* by M. Scott Peck, delaying gratification is a process of scheduling the pain and pleasure of life in such a way to as to enhance the pleasures by meeting and experiencing the pain first and getting it over with. It is the only decent way to live.

> ### *"But let patience have its perfect work, that you may be perfect and complete, lacking nothing."*
> *~James 1:4*

In my experience, you do one of two things in life: (1) You can pay the price now and enjoy later, or (2) you enjoy now and pay the price later. Regardless, you always pay a price.

Don't be caught by today's pleasures and blinded to the pain of tomorrow. You can pay today and enjoy life tomorrow, or you can enjoy life your way today and pay the price tomorrow with heavy interest. That, my friends, is hell on earth and eternal hell beyond.

> ### *"He is no fool who gives up what he cannot keep in order to gain what he cannot lose."*
> *~Jim Elliot*

ACTION PLAN

Chapter 5

- Make a list of pleasures you can give up for a brighter future. In other words, what sacrifices are you willing to make today to secure a better tomorrow?

- Name at least one thing you could be doing (that you are not currently doing) which would benefit your future.

- What is one step you can take to begin taking action on what you wrote above?

PSALM 86:5

For you, Lord,
are good,
and ready
to forgive.

6

FORGIVENESS

A Free Man Forgives

Problems do not go away. They must be
worked through or else they forever re-
main a barrier to the growth and develop-
ment of the spirit. Forgiveness is a key to
breaking through problems that are barriers in your life.

> *"Bear with each other*
> *and forgive whatever grievances*
> *you have against one another.*
> *Forgive as the Lord forgives you."*
> ~Colossians 3:13

If you cannot forgive your fellow man, how
do you expect our Lord and Savior to forgive you? When you forgive, you release
yourself of anger. You become free to pro-
ceed and enjoy the life that our Father in
Heaven has designed for you.

If you think you have been wronged, take the first step and tell this person that they are forgiven and forgive them indeed. In the same manner if you have wronged others, go and apologize to them and ask for their forgiveness. The relationship is always more important than the issue.

Do not judge or criticize others. He who is without fault should cast the first stone.

> *"Misunderstanding is never ended by an argument but by tact, diplomacy, conciliation and a sympathetic desire to see the other person's viewpoint."*
>
> **Dale Carnegie**

> *"Accept one another, then just as Christ accepted you, in order to bring praise to God."*
>
> **~Romans 15:7**

Accept people, situations, circumstances, and events as they occur. "Taking Responsibility" means not blaming anyone or anything for your situation. It means the ability to have a creative response to the situation as it is now.

If you creatively respond to people and situations based on the principles shared in this book, you will undoubtedly experience success. The favor you show will be returned to you, and the very situations that looked like barriers may very well open up into a wide door of opportunity.

> *"Do not judge, or you too will be judged,*
> *for in the same way you judge others,*
> *you will be judged,*
> *and with the measure you use,*
> *it will be measured to you."*
>
> ~*Matthew 7:1-2*

If you feel trapped by other people and always see your life being the result of what they are doing to you, take this advice to forgive seriously. Forgiveness is the key that will open the trap door.

Even if what others are doing to you is wrong, do not let that keep you from doing what is right. If you refuse to forgive, you are trapped just as they are. If you choose to forgive, you not only free yourself but have given them an opportunity to be free as well.

As the Bible says ...

> *And just as you want men to do to you,*
> *you also do to them likewise.*

But if you love those who love you,
what credit is that to you? For
even sinners love those who love them.

And if you do good to those
who do good to you,
what credit is that to you?
For even sinners do the same.

And if you lend to those
from whom you hope to receive back,
what credit is that to you?
For even sinners lend to sinners
to receive as much back.

But love your enemies, do good,
and lend, hoping for nothing in return;
and your reward will be great ...

~Luke 6:31-35

ACTION PLAN

Chapter 6

- Make a list of those who have wronged you. Pray for each person and forgive them. Remember, this is a decision and not a feeling. Choose to forgive them as our Lord forgives our trespasses.

- Approach the people on your list either in writing, with a phone call, or in person letting them know they are forgiven.

- Make a second list of people, this time list the people in your life whom you have wronged.

- Pray and ask for forgiveness. Approach these people and genuinely ask them for forgiveness.

Note:

Be sensitive to the Spirit of God as you approach people. Some people do not even know they have wronged you, and others may not want to revisit the issues. Regardless of their responses, choose the way of peace. Stand by your forgiveness of others and the forgiveness from the Lord toward you.

DEUTERONOMY
28:13

*You shall be
above only,
and not beneath.*

A WINNING ATTITUDE

Live in High Places

It has been said that your attitude determines your altitude. In other words, the height of achievement is directly related to your attitude.

What is attitude? It is the prophet of your future. It offers a glimpse of what is truly in your heart and what you are drawing to yourself. It grows from roots deep within and brings fruit out in the open. It broadcasts your substance and can draw people to you or repel them away from you. It can be your best friend or worst enemy.

The most important commandment that our Lord and Savior charged us with is to love one another and to love the Almighty God. The key word is love.

Having a winning attitude means to have a heart that exudes brotherly and sisterly love.

"Above all, love each other deeply
because love covers a multitude of sins."
~1 Peter 4:8

"Let nothing be done
through selfish ambition or conceit,
but in lowliness of mind
let each esteem others better than himself.
Let each of you look out
not only for his own interests,
but also for the interests of others."
~Philippians 2:3-4

To love one another means giving up our need to be right, being slow to anger, and being forgiving. Loving others means treating your fellow man the way you want to be treated.

"Love suffers long and is kind;
love does not envy;
love does not parade itself,
is not puffed up;
does not behave rudely,
does not seek its own,
is not provoked, thinks no evil;
does not rejoice in iniquity,
but rejoices in the truth;

bears all things, believes all things, hopes all things, endures all things. Love never fails."

~1 Corinthians 13:4-6a

I challenge you just for one week to treat every person you meet, <u>without exception</u>, as the most important person on earth. You will find that they will begin treating you the same way.

John Maxwell says, "Love people more than your opinions. Anyone who loves his opinions more than he does his friends will defend his opinions and destroy his friends." Forget yourself and give up your need to be right.

One of the principles I live by is to always remember that the issue I am facing is of less importance than my relationship with the people involved. What good is it for me to win an argument and lose a friend?

Dale Carnegie talks about the "3 Cs" of human relationship ... Do not criticize, condemn, or complain. Criticism is futile because it puts a person at odds with you and usually makes him strive to justify himself. The person's back is against a wall and he or she will become defensive.

Criticizing and condemning is bad because it wounds a person's precious pride, hurts his sense of importance and arouses resentment.

Don't harbor anger against your fellow man. By fighting you never get enough, but by yielding you get more than you expect. Hatred is never ended by hatred but by love.

Live your life with integrity. Integrity is doing what you say, when you say you will do it. Be a good role model to your kids, your brothers and sisters, peers and subordinates.

Alfred Adler in his book entitled "What Life Should Mean To You" says that "it is the individual who is not interested in his fellow man who has the greatest difficulties in life and provides the greatest injuries to others. It is from among such individuals that all human failures spring."

The Stanford Research Institute says that money made in any endeavor is determined only 12.5% by knowledge and 87.5% by your ability to deal with people.

Our attitude can turn problems into blessings. It's not what is happening to me, but my reaction to what happened that will make a difference. If I look at my circumstances as a curse, they will curse me. If I call it a blessing, it will bless me.

Step up and learn from your situation. My past is nothing more than the trail I have left behind. What drives my life is the energy that I generate in my present moment.

There are some of you reading this and thinking, "There is no way out. I am already too old." Maybe your past is not much to brag about. Maybe you have used the famous "if only" words: "If only...If only I was treated fairly... If only the government paid my arrear... If only you would have ..."

Maybe you have a right to use those words and if such is the case, I refer you to read Jesus' words, in John 3:6, ***"Human life comes from human parents, but spiritual life comes from the spirit."***

In other words, if you only live according to your humanity you will be limited. You must begin to live according to your spirit in order to tap into the spiritual life God has designed for you to live.

Make some choices, make a commitment, and take a risk. That's where the fruit is.

It's never too late. Stop making excuses about your past. Go for it! Don't allow circumstances or age limit you. Only you can limit yourself.

> *"So now you are not a slave;*
> *you are God's child,*
> *and God will give you*
> *the blessing He promised,*
> *because you are his child."*
>
> *~Galatians 4:7*

ACTION PLAN

Chapter 7

- For an entire week, treat every person you meet as the most important person in your life.

- Try, one day at a time, for a week to honor the "3 Cs" of relationships. Do not criticize, condemn or complain. The following poem may be an inspiration to you, especially concerning your relationships with children or other young people in your life.

- Make a list of your blessings, the things for which you are thankful.

CHILDREN LEARN WHAT THEY LIVE
~Dorothy Law Nolte

If a child lives with criticism,
He learns to condemn.
If a child lives with hostility,
He learns to fight.
If a child lives with ridicule,
He learns to be shy.
If a child lives with shame,
He learns to feel guilty.

If a child lives with tolerance,
He learns to be patient.
If a child lives with encouragement,
He learns confidence.
If a child lives with praise,
He learns to appreciate.
If a child lives with fairness,
He learns justice.

If a child lives with security,
He learns to have faith.
If a child lives with approval,
He learns to like himself.
If a child lives with acceptance and friendship,
He learns to find love in the world.

PROVERBS 4:7

*Wisdom is the
principal thing;
Therefore, get wisdom.*

PRIORITIES

Above All Things ...

Suppose you had a bank that credited
your account each morning with 1440
francs with one condition: the portion you
failed to use during the day would be
erased and no balance could be carried
over. What would you do? You'd draw out
every franc every day and use it to your
advantage.

Well, you do have such a bank and its
name is "time." Every morning you are
credited with 1440 minutes. The portion
you fail to invest to a good purpose is
written off as lost forever.

Look carefully then how you walk!
Live purposefully and worthily
and accurately,
not as the unwise and witless,
but as wise — sensible,

intelligent people;
Making the very most of the time —
buying up each opportunity —
because the days are evil.
~Ephesians 5:15-16 (Amplified Bible)

Folks! Do not waste your life. Wake up each morning with a goal and every day will be exciting - especially if that goal is part of your life purpose. Remember, you cannot do everything or be everywhere. You have to prioritize. Do the things that are meaningful and help get you closer to your goals first.

There are only 24 hours in a day, and we have only a short time to live on planet earth. Let's face it; we cannot do it all. Even Jesus, our Lord and Savior, did not try to do it all. In fact, that's one reason why the Holy Spirit was sent. Jesus could not be everywhere with everyone, but the Spirit of God could.

Jesus lived a life of priorities empowered by the Holy Spirit. Let us not deceive ourselves into thinking we can do it all! We have to program ourselves and our lives around our priorities.

One human endowment that differentiates us from other species is our power to execute an independent will, which is the ability to make decisions and choices based on beliefs of our choosing. We are constantly faced with situations demanding a decision or choice, each one planting a seed today that will grow into our future. Putting it differently, where we are today is a result of the choices and decisions we made yesterday.

Setting priorities is making a commitment with yourself to "walk the talk." It is programming yourself with the blueprints of success, a road map to making your dreams a reality. With the right programming, chances are you will make the right decision when faced with a choice.

The first place to start is to identify your personal priorities. For me, it is very simple: God first, family second, job third.

Some years ago when I was doing my specialty training, money was scarce and I had a family that was dependent upon me. I had an offer to work with another dentist in the evenings and on weekends. I had an appointment to meet with this doctor and start work. A week before the appointment, my nephew became sick and was admitted in the hospital in Atlanta. I was faced with the decision to keep my ap-

pointment and begin working or to cancel
my appointment and leave for Atlanta im-
mediately. I was restless, thinking about
what to do. Suddenly a still voice within
myself said, "Priorities." There was no
question about what to do because work is
subordinate to my family.

**"*Things which matter most must never be
at the mercy of things which matter least.*"**

~*Goethe*

ACTION PLAN

Chapter 7

- Write down five of your top priorities in order of importance.

- Make a list of your ten best friends. These are people you can count on to be there for you.

- Place these priorities and people at the top of your list when making decisions.

JOHN 3:16

*For God
so loved the world
that He gave ...*

EPILOGUE

The End … The Beginning

It is my sincere prayer that the Lord will bless you as you strive to live the life He promised you, and that you will develop a personal relationship with our Lord and Savior, Jesus Christ.

> *If you confess with your mouth the Lord Jesus and believe in your heart that God has raised Him from the dead, you will be saved.*
>
> *For with the heart one believes unto righteousness, and with the mouth confession is made unto salvation.*
>
> *~Romans 10:9-10*

I ask you now to stop and pray to God using the script as follows:

PRAYER

Dear Lord, I know that I am a sinner.
I ask you to forgive me of my sins.
I want to know you personally.
I believe that you sent your only son, Jesus
Christ, to die for my sins on the cross,
and I believe that you raised Jesus
from the dead.
I want to spend eternity with you.
Thank you for loving me.
Invite me into your kingdom.
Reveal to me the plans you have for me.
I pray in Jesus' name. Amen.

If you have earnestly and sincerely prayed this prayer, you can be assured of spending eternity with Him. Write to me so I can pray for you and send encouraging study material to you which can help you in your walk with the Lord.

Dr. Emmanuel Ngoh

3608 Wheeler Road
Augusta, GA 30909, USA
e-mail: success@augustaendo.com

Dr. Emmanuel C. Ngoh was born in Cameroon, West Africa. Though he was an unlikely candidate, he found the reality of success in God's plan for every man.

Despite economic circumstances, family hardships, and discouraging words from every side, Emmanuel pursued his goal of becoming a dentist and eventually traveled to the United States of America to acquire his training.

Through many events and acquaintances, God's hand was upon Emmanuel and he was able not only to realize his dream, but discover his specialty within the field of dentistry and acquire accolades and awards all along the way.

He has found success in his profession by remaining unconditionally committed to excellence as well as combining expertise with technology in an atmosphere that promotes Christ and uplifts people.

After experiencing God's plan for personal and professional success, Dr. Ngoh's passion is to help others discover their God-given potential and pursue their dreams successfully. His first book, "Principles of Success" is one way of doing just that.